THE 50 TOP SINGLES OF ALL TIME

GOLD EDITI

THE 50 TOP SINGLES OF ALL TIME GOLD EDITION

Wise Publications
part of The Music Sales Group
London / New York / Paris / Sydney / Copenhagen / Berlin / Madrid / Tokyo

Published by:
Wise Publications
8/9 Frith Street, London W1D 3JB, England.

Exclusive distributors:
Music Sales Limited
Distribution Centre, Newmarket Road,
Bury St. Edmunds Suffolk IP33 3YB, England.
Music Sales Pty Limited
120 Rothschild Avenue, Rosebery, NSW 2018, Australia.

Order No. AM977086
ISBN 1-84449-022-X

Compiled by Nick Crispin.
Music arrangements by Jack Long.
Music processed by Paul Ewers Music Design.
Photographs courtesy of London Features International.

Printed and bound in Malta by Interprint Limited.

www.musicsales.com

All I Have To Do Is Dream

Words & Music by Boudleaux Bryant

1.
2.
E♭ Cm A♭ B♭ E♭ Cm
ev - er I want you all I have to do is dream,
ev - er I want you all I have to do is
A♭ B♭ E♭ A♭ E♭ E♭7
dream, dream, dream. When dream.
A♭ Gm Fm E♭ E♭7
I can make you mine, taste your lips of wine, a - ny time, night or day.
mf
A♭ Gm F7
On - ly trou - ble is, gee whiz, I'm dream - ing my life a -
cresc.
f

Fm7/B♭ B♭ E♭ Cm A♭ B♭ E♭ Cm
- way! I need you so that I could die, I love you so
mp
A♭ B♭ E♭ Cm A♭ B♭
and that is why, when - ev - er I want you all I have to do is
1. E♭ A♭ E♭ E♭7
dream.
2. E♭ Cm
dream,
rit.
A♭ B♭ E♭ Cm A♭ B♭ E♭
dream, dream, dream, dream, dream, dream, dream, dream.
4fr 6fr 3fr

Angie

Words & Music by Mick Jagger & Keith Richards

Am E7 G F
(Instrumental on 𝄋)
Angie, Angie, where will it lead us from
B♭/F F G C G Dm Am
here? (1. + 𝄋) With no loving in our souls and no money in our coats,
(Verse 3 see block lyric)
C F G Am
To Coda
you can't say we're satisfied. But Angie,
D.𝄋. al Coda
E7 G F B♭/F F G C E7
Angie, you can't say we've never tried.

Coda
Dm
Am
An - gie, I still love you ba - by,
Dm
Am
ev - 'ry - where I look I see your eyes.
Dm
Am
There ain't a wo - man who comes close to you,
C
F
G
come on ba - by dry your eyes.
But

Verse 2:
Angie you're beautiful
But ain't it time we said goodbye?
Angie I still love you
Remember all those night we cried?
All the dreams we held so close
Seemed to all go up in smoke
Let me whisper in your ear
Angie Angie
Where will it lead us from here?

Verse: 3
Instrumental
Oh Angie don't you weep
Ah your kisses still taste sweet
I hate that sadness in your eyes
But Angie Angie
Ain't it time we said goodbye?

Babylon

Words & Music by David Gray

E♭maj9/G
A♭maj7
E♭maj9/G
to red.
Turn-in' ov - er T. V. sta - tions,
A♭maj7
E♭maj9/G
A♭maj7
si - tu - a - tions run-nin' through my head.
E♭maj9
A♭add9
B♭11
Look-in' back through time you know it's clear that I've been blind, I've been a
E♭maj9
A♭add9
B♭11
E♭maj9
fool
to op - en up my heart to all that

A♭add9
B♭11
E♭maj9
jea-lous - y, that bit-ter - ness, that ri - di-cule.
E♭
B♭
Fm7
An' if you want it, come an' get it, for cry-in' out loud.
Gm7
The love that I was giv-in' you was
nev-er in doubt.
Ab
Let go your heart,

B♭
Fm7
B♭7
B♭6
let go your head and feel it now.
E♭
fr3
B♭
Fm7
Let go your heart, let go your head and feel it
1.
B♭
E♭
fr3
A♭maj7
now, Ba - by - lon. Ba - by - lon.
E♭
fr3
A♭maj7
2.
B♭7
B♭6
now.

E♭
B♭
Fm7
fr3
Let go your heart, let go your head and feel
B♭
E♭
B♭
it. Let go your heart, let go your head
Fm7
B♭
and feel it now, Ba - by - lon.
E♭
A♭maj9
fr5
E♭
Ba - by - lon.
Con pedale

Verse 2:
Saturday an' I'm runnin' wild
An' all the lights are changin' red to green
Movin' through the crowds, I'm pushin'
Chemicals are rushin' in my bloodstream
Only wish that you were here
You know I'm seein' it so clear
I've been afraid to show you how I really feel
Admit to some o' those bad mistakes I've made.

Well, if you want it come an' get it *etc.*

China In Your Hand

Words & Music by Carol Decker & Ronald Rogers

B♭ F/A Gm D/F♯
It was a flight on the wings of a young girl's dreams that
Gm7/F E♭maj7 F11
flew too far a - way.
E♭ F B♭ F/A Gm7 Dm/F
Don't push too far, your dreams are chi - na in your hand.
E♭ F Dm E♭maj7 F
Don't wish too hard be - cause they may come true and you can't help them.

E♭ F B♭ F/A
You don't know what you might have set up - on your - self.
Gm7 Dm/F E♭ E♭maj7 F11
Chi - na in your hand.
rit.
B♭ F E♭ B♭ F E♭ B♭ F E♭
In your hand, your hand.
8vb
a tempo
B♭ E♭ F B♭ F/A Gm7 Dm/F
Saxophone
(8vb)

Verse 2:
Come from greed, never born o' the seed.
Took a life from a barren land
Oh, eyes wide like a child in the form of man
A prophecy for a fantasy
The curse of a vivid mind.

Don't push too far *etc.*

Dance Away

Words & Music by Bryan Ferry

A♭ 4fr.
B♭
E♭
I said, "It's love." You said, "All right." It's fun - ny how
all to - geth - er, all a - lone. All at once
off the street on - to the floor. There was I,
Cm 3fr.
A♭ 4fr.
I could nev - er cry un - til to - night, and
my whole world had changed. Now I'm in the dark,
man - y times a fool. I hope and pray, but
B♭
A♭ 4fr.
B♭
you passed by hand in hand with an - oth - er guy.
off the wall. Let the strobe light up them all.
not too much. Out of reach is out of touch.

A♭
4 fr.
B♭
F
You're dressed to kill, and guess who's dy - ing?
I close my eyes and dance till dawn.
All the way is far e - nough.
Dance a-way the heart -
Dm
B♭
C
ache; dance a - way the tears.
F
Dm
B♭
To Coda
Dance a-way the heart - ache; dance a - way the tears.
1. C
B♭
Dance a - way.
2. C

F
D♭maj7
4 fr.
F
Dance a - way.
Dance a - way.
D♭maj7
4 fr.
G♭
F♭
Dance a - way.
D. S. 𝄋 al Coda
Coda
C
Repeat and fade
F
Dance a-way the heart -
Repeat and fade
Dm
B♭
C
ache; dance a - way the tears.

Can't Get You Out Of My Head

Words & Music by Cathy Dennis & Rob Davis

Dm
Am9
can't get you out of my head. Boy your lov - ing is all I
1° tacet
Dm
think a - bout. I just can't get you out of my head. Boy, it's
Am9
1.
2. 3.
more than I dared to think a - bout. think a - bout.
B♭maj7
A
G♯dim7
A
Ev - 'ry night, e - ve - ry day.
(2° see block lyric)

Gm7
3fr
Asus4
A
To Coda
Just to be there in your arms, Won't you
Dm
Am9
stay?
Dm
Won't you lay
Am9
B♭maj7
Stay for ev - er and

Am
D.%. al Coda
ev - er and ev - er and ev - er.
Coda
Dm
Am9
free.
Dm
Feel the need in
Am9
me
Dm
Set me free.

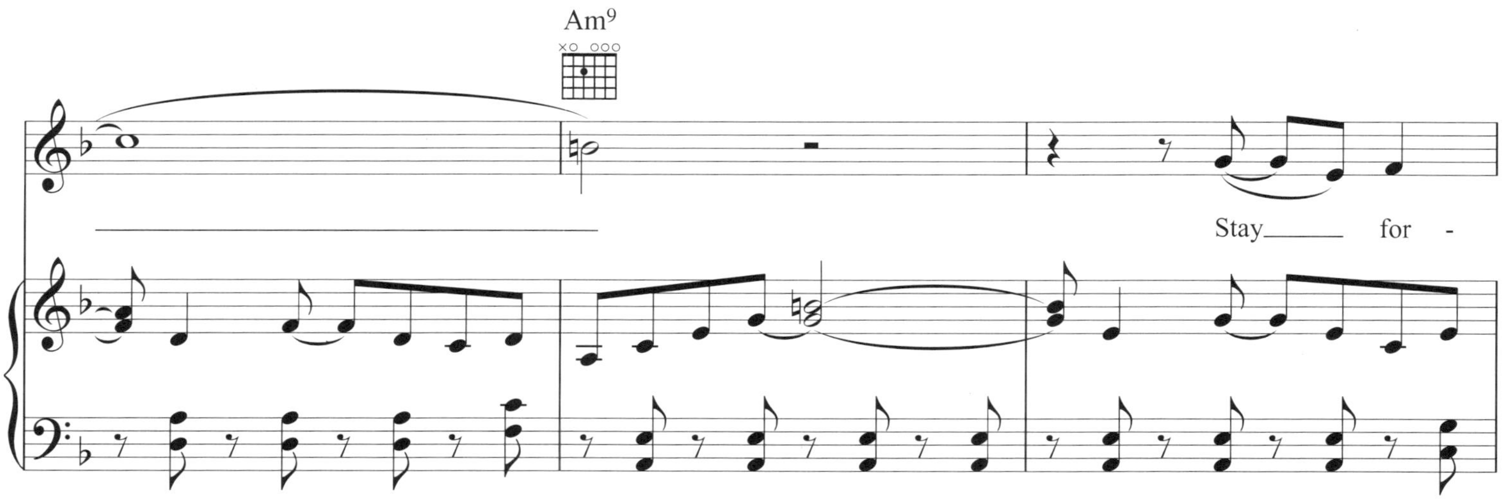

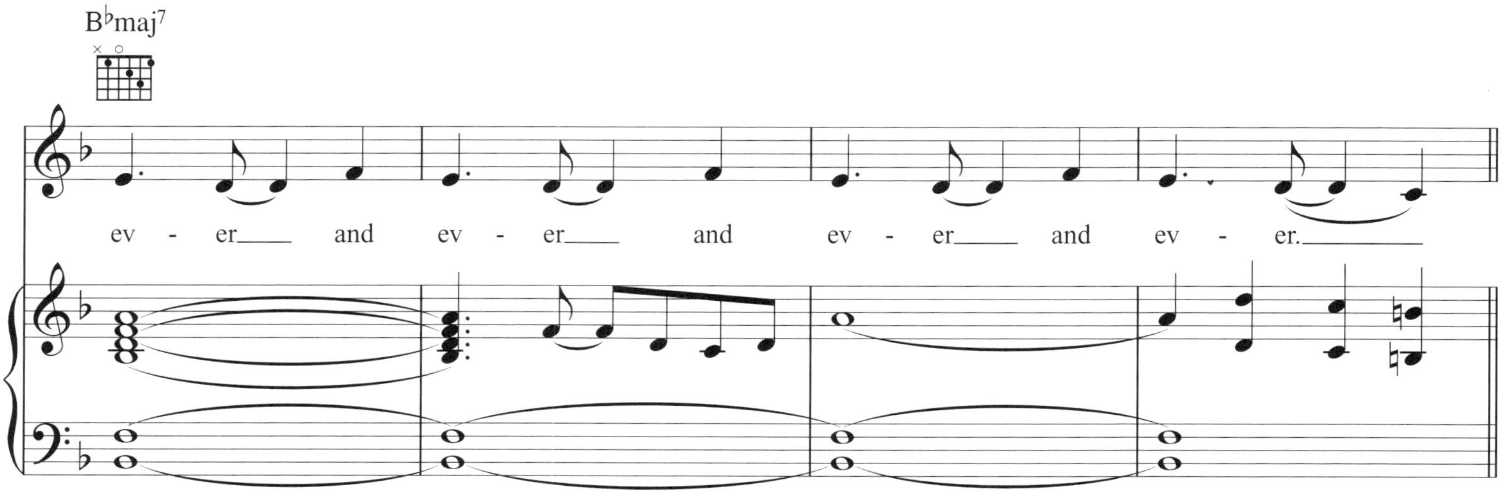

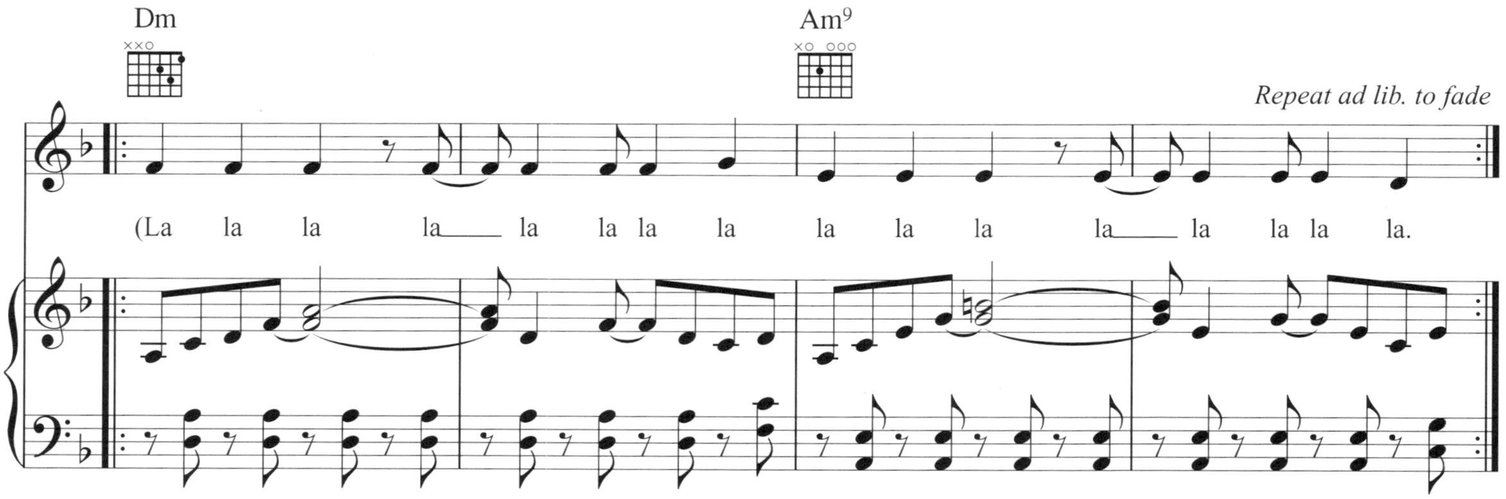

Verse 2:
There's a dark secret in me
Don't leave me locked in your heart
Set me free *etc.*

Evergreen

Words & Music by Jörgen Elofsson, Per Magnusson & David Kreuger

G Dm7 C G
look at me like that, what you're think - ing, what's be - hind. Don't tell me, but it
Dm7 C/E Fadd9 G C
feels like love. I'm gon - na take this mo - ment and make it last for - ev -
G F
- er. I'm gon - na give my heart a - way and pray we'll stay to - ge -
Gsus4 G C
- ther. 'Cause you're the one good rea - son, you're the on - ly girl
3

G
Dm7
C/E
that I need; 'cause you're more beau-ti-ful than I have ev-er seen,
F
C/E
Dm7
G11
1.
oh yeah. I'm gon-na take this night and make it ev-er-green.
2.
C
G
Am
F
We can make it last for ev-er more.
C
G
Dm7
C
Fadd9
N.C.
Don't tell me that it feels like love. I'm gon-na take this

D
A
mo - ment_ and make it last for ev - er.3_____ I'm gon - na give my heart_
G
Asus4
A
__ a - way_ and pray_ we'll stay_ to - ge - ther. 'Cause you're the one good
D
A
rea - son,_ you're the on - ly girl_____ that I need;_ 'cause you're more
1.
G
Asus4
A
beau - ti - ful__ than I__ have ev - er seen._ I'm gon - na take this

Verse 2:
Touch like an angel
Like velvet to my skin
And I wonder
I wonder why you wanna stay the night
What you're dreaming
What's behind.
Don't tell me, but it feels like love.

I'm gonna take this moment *etc.*

Eternal Flame

Words & Music by Billy Steinberg, Tom Kelly & Susanna Hoffs

B7
Em7
A7
To Coda
Do you feel the same? Am I only
Do you feel the same? Am I only
D
Bm7
1.
Am7
dreaming, is this burning
dreaming or
2.
Am7
an eternal flame? is this burning an eternal flame?
D
Dm7
G/D
D
Say my name, sun shines through the rain, a whole
f

F G C G/B Am7 C/G
life so lone - ly, and then come and ease the pain.
D Bm7 F/C C
1.
D sus2 D
I don't wan - na lose this feel - ing, oh.
Em B Em A7 D Bm7
Am7
2.
D sus2
D.%. al Coda
(Repeat verse 1)
oh.

Coda
D Bm7 Am7
dream - ing or is this burn - ing an e - ter - nal flame?
G Em7 C D G Em7
Close your eyes, give me your hand, darl - ing. Do you feel my heart beat-
f
C D7sus4 Em B Em7 A7
- ing? Do you un - der - stand? Do you feel the same? Am I on - ly
D Bm7 Am7
Repeat to fade
dream - ing, is this burn - ing an e - ter - nal flame?

The First Cut Is The Deepest

Words & Music by Cat Stevens

C G F G C G
tak - en just all___ that I had,___ but if you want, I'll___ try___ to love a - gain.
sure gon - na give you a try,___ and if you want, I'll___ try___ to love a - gain.
F G C F G
Ba - by, I'll try___ to love a - gain but I know.___
Ba - by, I'll try___ to love a - gain but I know.___
C G F G C G
The first cut is the deep - est; ba - by, I know___ the first cut is the deep -

F G C G F G
-est. When it comes to be-in' luck-y she's cursed; when it
1.
C F G
comes to lov-in' me she's worse.
2.
C G
2.I still comes to lov-in' me she's worse.
F G C F G
Repeat and fade

Great Balls Of Fire

Words & Music by Otis Blackwell & Jack Hammer

C7
thought it was fun - ny. You came a - long and moved me, hon - ey.
D7 C7 G
I changed my mind, this love is fine. Good - ness gra - cious, great
C7 G
balls of fire! Kiss me, ba - by, Oh, yo! It feels good.
C7 D7
Hold me, ba - by. I want to love you like a lov - er should.

D7 N.C.
You're fine, so kind. I'm gon - na tell the world that you're
D7 G
mine, mine, mine, mine. I chew my nails and I twid - dle my thumbs.
C7 D7
I'm real nerv - ous but it sure is fun! Oh, ba - by, you're
C7 G N.C. 1. 2. G
driv - in' me cra - zy. Good - ness gra - cious, great balls of Fire! balls of fire!
f
mf

God Only Knows

Words & Music by Brian Wilson & Tony Asher

E/B
B♭m7(♭5)
A
I'll make you so sure about it. God only knows
To Coda
E/G♯
F♯m7
1.
E
what I'd be without you.
2.
A/E
G
N.C.
A/E
G
N.C.
G/D
Em6
Bm/F♯
Bm7
Ah, ah. Do do do do do do

E/D
A/E
Fdim7
do. Ba ba ba ba ba ba ba ba ba ba ba ba ba ba ba
A/E
D♯m7(♭5)
D
ba ba ba ba ba ooh. And God on - ly knows
A/C♯
Bm7
D.%. al Coda
Coda
F♯m7
what I'd be with - out you.
you.
E/G♯
A
E/G♯
And God on - ly knows what I'd be with - out

Verse 2:
If you should ever leave me
Though life would still go on, believe me
The world could show nothing to me
So what good would living do me?
God only knows what I d be without you.

Verse 3 as Verse 2

Golden Brown

Words & Music by Jean-Jacques Burnel, Jet Black,
Hugh Cornwell & David Greenfield

E♭m D♭ E♭m D♭ E♭m D♭ E♭m D♭
Gold - en Brown, tex - ture like sun, lays me down,
(Verses 2 & 3 see block lyric)
E♭m D♭ E♭m D♭ E♭m D♭
with my mind she runs through - out the night. No need to fight,
To Coda
1.
E♭m D♭ E♭m D♭ E♭m D♭ E♭m D♭
nev - er a frown with Gol - den Brown.

2.
D.C. al Coda
CODA
E♭m D♭ E♭m D♭ B♭m Fm
with Gol - den Brown.
G♭ D♭ B♭m Fm G♭ D♭
B♭m Fm G♭ D♭ B♭m Fm
A♭ 4fr G♭ E♭m D♭ E♭m D♭ E♭m D♭
1st time — Instrumental
2nd time — Ad lib. vocal

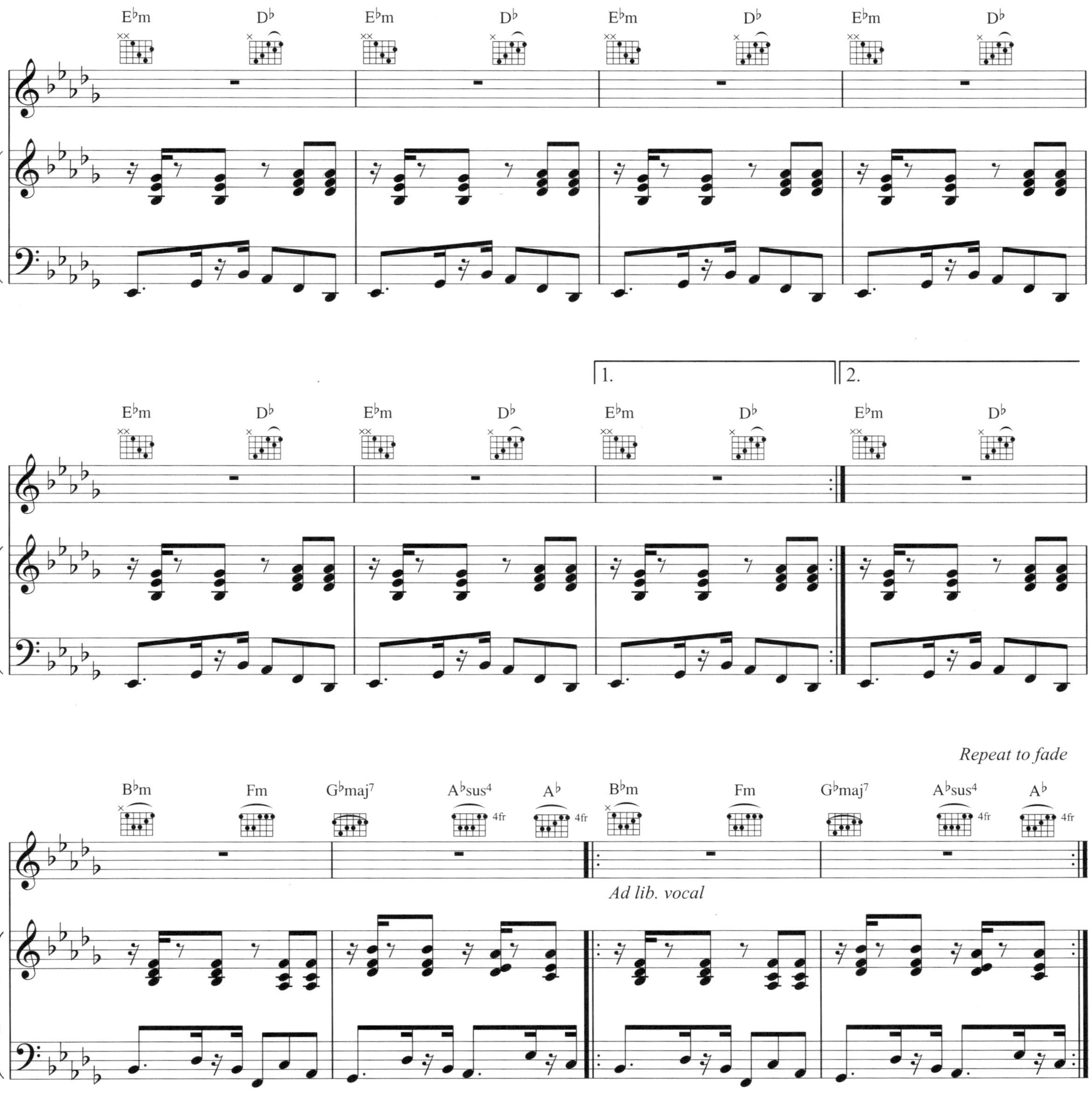

Verse 2:
Every time just like the last.
On her ship, tied to the mast
To distant lands, takes both my hands.
Never a frown with Golden Brown.

Verse 3:
Golden Brown, finer temptress
Through the ages she's heading west
From far away, stays for a day.
Never a frown with Golden Brown.

He Ain't Heavy, He's My Brother

Words by Bob Russell
Music by Bobby Scott

F
Am7
D7
Am7
where, who knows where? But I'm
bear, well get there. For I
there, why not share. And the
f
G
D/F♯
Em
3
strong, strong e - nough to car - - ry
know he would not en - cum - - ber
load does - n't weigh me down at
3
E♭
3fr
G
Am7
To Coda
him.
me. He ain't hea - vy, he's my
all.

G
1. Am7
2. Am7
G7/B
brother.
So on we
If I'm
C
D/C
C
laden at all,
I'm laden with
D/C
Bm
Dm
sadness that everyone's heart isn't
Cmaj7
B7
Em
G7/D
C
C/B
filled with the gladness of love

A9
6fr
Am7/D
D7
D.S. al Coda
for one an - oth - er.
It's a long, long
CODA
G
Am7/D
G
bro - ther,
He's my
choir
bro - ther.
D/F♯
Em
Am7/D
He ain't
G
D/F♯
C
D7
Repeat and fade
choir
hea - vy,
he's my
bro - ther.
He ain't

Help!

Words & Music by John Lennon & Paul McCartney

F♯m
D
G
I nev - er need - ed an - y - bod - y's help in an - y way
My in - de - pen - dence seems to van - ish in the haze
A
C♯m
4fr
But now these days are gone, I'm not so self - as - sured,
But ev - 'ry now and then I feel so in - se - cure,
F♯m
Now I find I've changed my mind, I've
I know that I just need you like I've
D
G
A
Bm
o - pened up the doors.
nev - er done be - fore.
Help me if you can, I'm feel - ing

Bm/A
G
down,
And I do ap - pre - ci - ate you be - ing round
E7
Help me get my feet back on the ground
A
Won't you please, please help me?
1.
3.
A
F♯m
A
A6
Help me, help me! Ooh.

I Say A Little Prayer

Words by Hal David
Music by Burt Bacharach

Medium tempo

C♯7 F♯m7 Bm7
While comb - ing my hair now
R.H.
E A
and won - d'ring what dress to wear now. I
D C♯7
say a lit - tle prayer for you. For -
D E9 C♯m7 F♯m7 G6 A A9
ev - er, for - ev - er you'll stay in my heart and I will love you for -

D
E9
C♯m7
4fr
F♯m7
ev - er and ev - er we nev - er will part, oh
D/F♯
F♯m7
A9
A
D
E9
how Ill love you, to - geth - er, to - geth - er, thats
C♯m7
4fr
F♯m7
G6
A
A9
how it must be. To live with - out you would
1. Smoothly
D
D6
C♯
4fr
on - ly mean heart - break for me.
mf

2. Smoothly
C♯
4fr
F♯m7
me.
My dar - ling be -
mf
p
R.H.
Bm7
D/E
lieve me,
for me there is
no one
mp
Amaj7
E9sus4
but
you.
Please love me
Amaj7
E9sus4
too.
I'm in love with

Verse 2:
I run for the bus, dear.
While riding, I think of us dear.
I say a little prayer for you.
At work I just take time,
And all through my coffee break time
I say a little prayer for you.

Forever, forever, *etc.*

I Get The Sweetest Feeling

Words & Music by Van McCoy & Alicia Evelyn

B♭ Gsus4 G E♭maj7 Fm7/B♭
you. When you turn on your smile
E♭maj7 Fm7/B♭ D♭maj7
I feel my heart go wild. I'm like a child
fr4
G♭ Fsus4 F
with a brand new toy. And I get the
B♭ Fm7/B♭ B♭
sweet-est feel-ing, hon-ey the sweet-est. (Sweet-est feel-

Fm7
B♭
Fm7
- ing.) Ba - by the sweet - est, (sweet - est feel - ing) lov - ing you.
To Coda
1.
2.
Gsus4
G
Gsus4
G
C
Gsus4
G
C
Yeah.
C
B♭
C
B♭
C
B♭
Asus4
A
Gsus4
G
D.%. al Coda
Mm.

Verse 2:
The warmer your kiss, the deeper you touch me baby
The deeper your touch, the more you thrill me
It's more than I can stand girl
When you hold my hand
I feel so grand that I could cry.

And I get the (sweetest feeling)
Mama the sweetest (sweetest feeling)
Baby the sweetest (sweetest feeling)
Loving you.

Verse 3:
The greater your love, the stronger you hold me baby
The stronger your hold, the more I need you
With every passing day
I love you more in every way
I'm in love to stay and I wanna say.

I get the (sweetest feeling)
Baby the sweetest (sweetest feeling)
Honey the sweetest (sweetest feeling)
Loving you.

The Israelites

Words & Music by Desmond Dacres & Leslie Kong

Moderate shuffle
B♭
Get up in the morn - ing, slav - ing for bread sir, so that a e - ver - ry mouth
mf
B♭7
E♭
6fr
F
can be fed. Poor me,
B♭
D♭
4fr
B♭
Is - rael - ite. My wife and my kids, they packed
B♭7
up and they leave me; "Dar - ling," she said, "I was yours to re - ceive."

E♭ 6fr
F
B♭
Poor me, Is - rael - ite.
D♭ 4fr
B♭
Shirt, them I tear up trou - sers are gone; I
B♭7
E♭ 6fr
don't want to end up like Bon - nie and Clyde.
3
Poor
F
B♭
D♭ 4fr
me, Is - rael - ite.

B♭
Af - ter a storm there must be a calm - ing. They catch me in the farm, you
B♭7
E♭
6fr
F
To Coda
sound the a - larm. Poor me,
B♭
D♭
4fr
B♭
Is - rael - ite. Yee.
D♭
4fr
B♭
E♭
6fr
B♭

D♭
B♭
F
D.S. al Coda
I said, I
Coda
B♭
B♭7
E♭
Is - rael - ite. Yee.
Poor, a poor, a
F
1.
B♭
B♭7
poor, a poor me, Is - rael - ite. I a won - der who I'm work - ing for?
2.
B♭
B♭7
D.S.S. and fade
Is - rael - ite. I look a down and out sir.

It Must Be Love

Words & Music by Labi Siffre

Am
Amadd9/E
Am
And I nev - er thought I'd feel this way, the way I feel
Amadd9/E
G
C/G
a - bout you.
G
Cmaj7
D
Em
Soon as I wake
I've got to be near
A7
Dm
E7
up ev - 'ry night, ev - 'ry day,
you ev - 'ry night, ev - ry day,

Am
C/G
D9/F#
D
I know that it's you I need to take the blues a-way.
I could-n't be hap-py a-ny oth-er way.
G
Bm
C
D
It must be love, love, love.
To Coda 2
G
Bm
C
D
C
It must be love, love, love. No-thing more,
D
C/E
To Coda 1
no-thing less: love is the best.

Am
Em
Am
Em
How can it be that we can say so much with-out
G
C
D5
5fr
G
C
D5
5fr
words?
Am
Em
Am
Em
3
Bless you and bless me, bless the bees and the
D.S. al Coda 1
G
C
D5
5fr
G
C
D5
5fr
N.C.
birds.

Coda 1
Am
G
C
G
1.
C
2.
D.S. al Coda 2
C
D
Coda 2
C
D
C
love.
Repeat to fade
G
Bm
C
D
It must be love, love, love

It's Oh So Quiet

Words & Music by Hans Lang, Bert Reisfeld & Erich Meder

Edim7
Fm7
B♭
B♭7/F
sshhhh... sshhhh... You're all a - lone
Medium 'swing' ♩=130
Edim7
Fm7
B♭7
E♭
B♭7(♯9)
E♭9
sshhhh... sshhhh... and so peace - ful un - til
cresc.
f
N.C.
A♭
B♭m9
A♭/C
D♭6
B♭7/D
You fall in love, zing boom. The sky up a -
E♭
E9(♯11)
E♭
C7
1.
F
D♭dim
F13
bove, zing boom, Ê is cav - ing in, Ê wow bam.

B♭9
N.C.
B9(♭5)
N.C.
You've never been so nuts about a guy; you wan-na laugh you wan-na cry; you
F9(♭5)
N.C.
Tempo 1°
B♭9
N.C.
cross your heart and hope to die 'til it's ov-er. And
2.
F
B13
B♭9
rit.
Tempo 1°
E♭
fr3
wow bam, of fall-ing in love?
p
Gm/D
A♭/C
B♭
E♭
fr3

Gm/D
B♭
E♭
It's
oh
so
quiet,
(Verse 4 see block lyric)
8va
(quasi celeste)
Gm/D
E♭6
Gm7
G♭dim
B♭7/F
it's
oh
so
still.
8va
Edim7
B♭7/F
B♭
2° only
(sshhhh...)
(sshhhh...)
You're
all
a -
8va
B9(♯11)
B♭7
2° only
lone
(sshhhh...)
(sshhhh...)
and
so
8va

1.
Tempo 2°
E♭ B♭7(♯9) E♭9 N.C. A♭ B♭m9
peace - ful un - till you ring the bell, bim bam.
8va
cresc.
f
A♭/C D♭6 B♭7/D E♭ E9(♯11) E♭ C7 F D♭dim
You shout and you yell, hi ho ho. You broke the spell.
F9 B♭9 N.C. B9(♭5) N.C.
Gee this is swell, you al - most have a fit; this guy is gorge' and I got hit. There's
F9(♭5) N.C. B♭9 N.C.
no mis - take: THIS IS IT! 'til it's ov - er. And

2.
Tempo 2°
E♭ B♭7(♯9) E♭9 N.C. A♭ B♭m9 A♭/C D♭6 B♭7/D
ri - ot. You blow a fuse, zing boom; the de - vil cuts
E♭ E9(♯11) E♭ C7 F B13
loose, zing boom. So what's the use, wow bam,
B♭9 E♭ E♭6 D♭ E♭6
of fall - ing in love? The
Fm9 A♭m9 B♭m9
sky caves in, the de - vil cuts loose; you blow, blow, blow,

Verse 2:
And then it's nice and quiet.
But soon again starts another big riot.
You blow a fuse, zing boom,
The devil cuts loose, zing boom.
So what's the use, wow bam,
Of falling in love?

Verse 4:
And then it's nice and quiet.
But soon again starts another big riot.

Knockin' On Heaven's Door

Words & Music by Bob Dylan

G
D
C
I feel like I'm knock - in' on hea - ven's door.
I feel like I'm knock - in on hea - ven's door.
G
D
Am7
Knock, knock, knock - in' on hea - ven's door.
G
D
C
Knock, knock, knock - in' on hea - ven's door.

G
D
Am7
Knock, knock, knock-in' on hea-ven's door
G
D
1.
C
2.
C
Knock, knock, knock-in' on hea-ven's door.
G
D
Am7
Repeat and fade
mp

Knowing Me, Knowing You

Words & Music by Benny Andersson, Björn Ulvaeus & Stig Anderson

Asus4
A
Asus4
A
tears in my eyes.
child-ren would play.
G
Bmadd9
This is where the sto-ry ends,
this is good-bye.
Now there's on-ly emp-ti-ness,
no-thing to say,
Bm
G
A
Know-ing me, know-ing you,
there is no-thing we can do.
D
G
A
Know-ing me know-ing you,
we just have to face it, this time

D G A D F♯m
— we're through. Break - in' up is ne - ver
G A D G A
ea - sy I know, but I have to go. Know - ing
D Gmaj7 A To Coda D Bm
2fr
me, know - ing you, it's the best I can do.
F♯m G A

D
Bm
F♯m
G
A
A
Bm
A
Bm
D.𝄋 al Coda
G
Know-ing me, know-ing
⊕ CODA
D
Bm
do.
F♯m
G
A
repeat and fade

Like A Prayer

Words & Music by Madonna & Pat Leonard

Bb F/A F/D Gm/D F
I'm down on my knees, I wan-na take you there. In the mid-night hour
C Bb F/A F/D Gm/D
I can feel your pow-er just like a prayer. You know I'll take you
Bb F C Dm
there. I hear your voice, it's like an an-gel sigh-ing.
there. Like a child you whis-per soft-ly to me.
Bb F C
I have no choice, I hear your voice, feels like fly-ing.
You're in con-trol. Just like a child, now I'm dan-cing.

B♭
F
C
Dm
I close my eyes. Oh God, I think I'm fall - ing
It's like a dream, no end and no be - gin - ning.
B♭
F
C
out of the sky. I close my eyes. Heav - en help me.
You're here with me, it's like a dream. Let the choir sing.
F
C
B♭
When you call my name it's like a lit - tle prayer. I'm down on my knees,
F/A
F/D
Gm/D
F
C
I wan - na take you there. In the mid - night hour I can feel your pow -

Bb
1. F/A
F/D
Gm/D
2. F/A
F/D
Gm/D
er just like a prayer. You know I'll take you. You know I'll take you
F
C
Bb
there. When you call my name it's like a lit-tle prayer. I'm down on my knees,
there. In the mid-night hour I can feel your pow-er just like a prayer.
F/A
F/D
Gm/D
Dm
C/D
Dm
I wan-na take you there.
You know I'll take you
C/D
Dm
C/D
Life is a mys-ter-y.

Dm
C/D
Dm
Ev - ery - one must stand a - lone. I hear you
C/E
Gm/B♭
F/A
B♭
F/C
C
call my name and it feels like
C/D
home. Just like a prayer your voice can take me there,
Dm
C/D
Just like a muse to me. You are a mys - ter - y.

Dm
C
Gm/Bb
Just like a dream _ you are not what you _ seem. _
F/A
Bb
F/C
C
_ Just like a prayer, _ no choice, your voice can take me
F
C
No Chord
there. (Just like a prayer _ I'll _ take you there. _
Bb
F/A
1. 2. 3.
Dm
4.
Dm
It's like a dream _ to me. _)
_)

Dm
C/D
Dm
(there.) Just like a prayer your voice can take me there. Just like a muse to me.
C/D
Dm
C/E
Gm/B♭
You are a mys- ter- y. Just like a dream you are not what you seem.
Repeat and fade
F/A
B♭
F/C
C
Dm
Just like a prayer, no choice your voice can take me there.
C/D
Dm
C/D
Your voice can take me there. Take me

Live Forever

Words & Music by Noel Gallagher

Em7
D
1, 4. May - be I just want to fly, I want to live, I don't want to
(Chorus 2 see block lyric)
Am7
C
D
die. May - be I just want to breathe, may - be I just don't be - lieve.
Em7
D
May - be you're the same as me, we see things they'll nev - er
Am7
F
1, 2, 3.
see, you and I are gon - na live for - ev - er.
I said

Chorus 2:
Maybe I will never be
All the things that I want to be.
Now is not the time to cry,
Now's the time to find out why.
I think you're the same as me,
We see things they'll never see,
You and I are gonna live forever.

Livin' La Vida Loca

Words & Music by Desmond Child & Robi Rosa

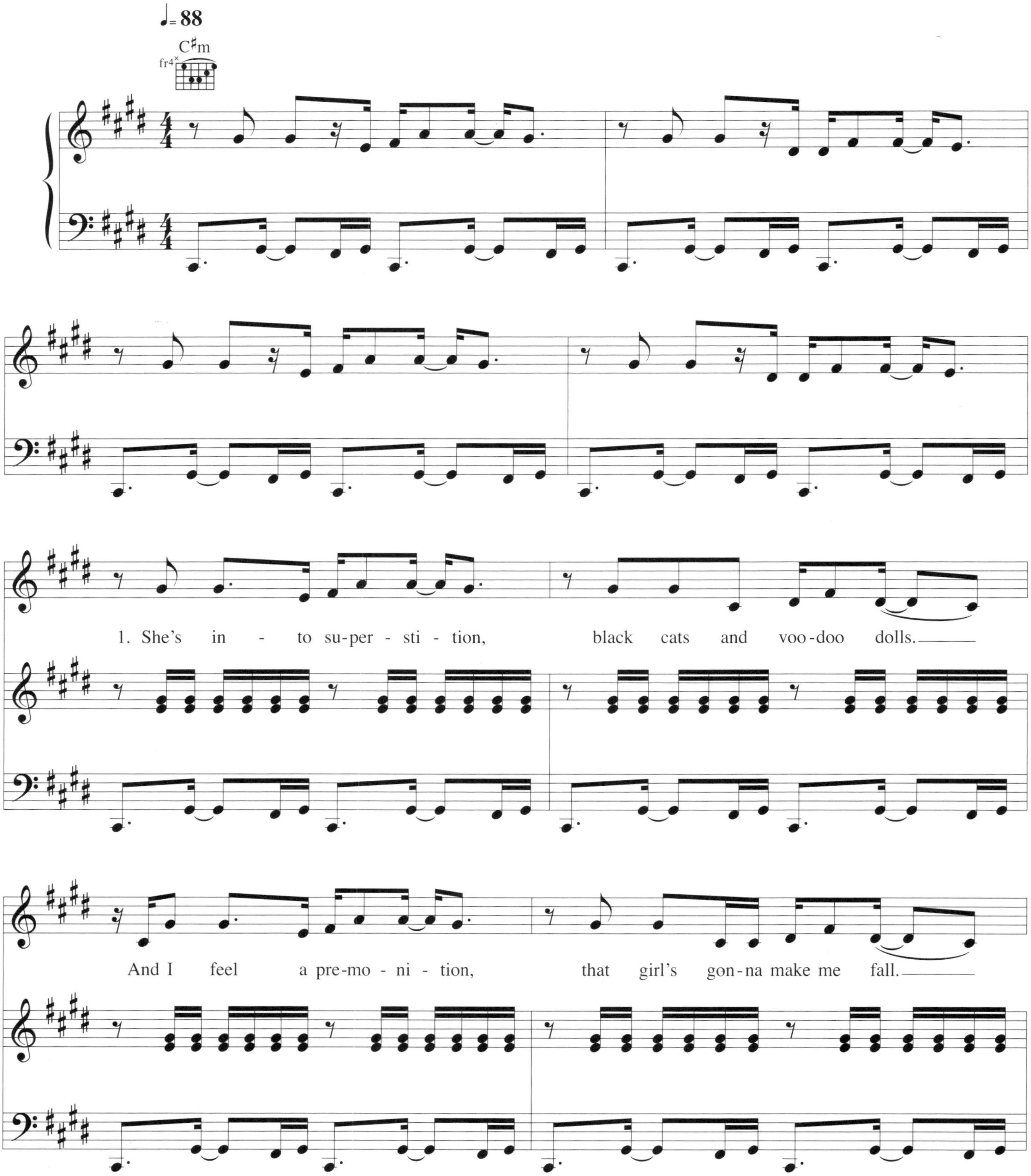

C♯m
fr4
2. She's in - to new sen - sa - tions, new kicks in the can-dle - light.
(Verse 3 see block lyric)
She's got a new ad - dic - tion s'full ev - 'ry day and night. She'll
F♯m
G♯m
fr4
make you take your clothes off and go dan - cing in the rain. She'll make

A
B
you live her crazy life or she'll take away your pain like a bul-
[G♯]
C♯m
-let to your brain. Upside inside out, she's
Badd9
C♯m
liv-in' la vi-da lo-ca. She'll push and pull you down,
Badd9
C♯m
liv-in' la vi-da lo-ca. Her lips are de-vil red and her

B add9
C♯m
skin's the col - our of moc - ca.
She will— wear— you out,—
B add9
C♯m
B add9
C♯m
liv-in' la vi - da lo - ca.
Liv-in' la vi - da lo - ca,
she's
B add9
C♯m
1.
liv - in' la vi - da lo - ca.

2.
F♯m
She'll make you take your clothes off and go dan-
G♯m
fr4
-cing in the rain.
A
She'll make you live her cra - zy life or she'll take
B
away your pain
[G♯]
like a bul - let to your brain.

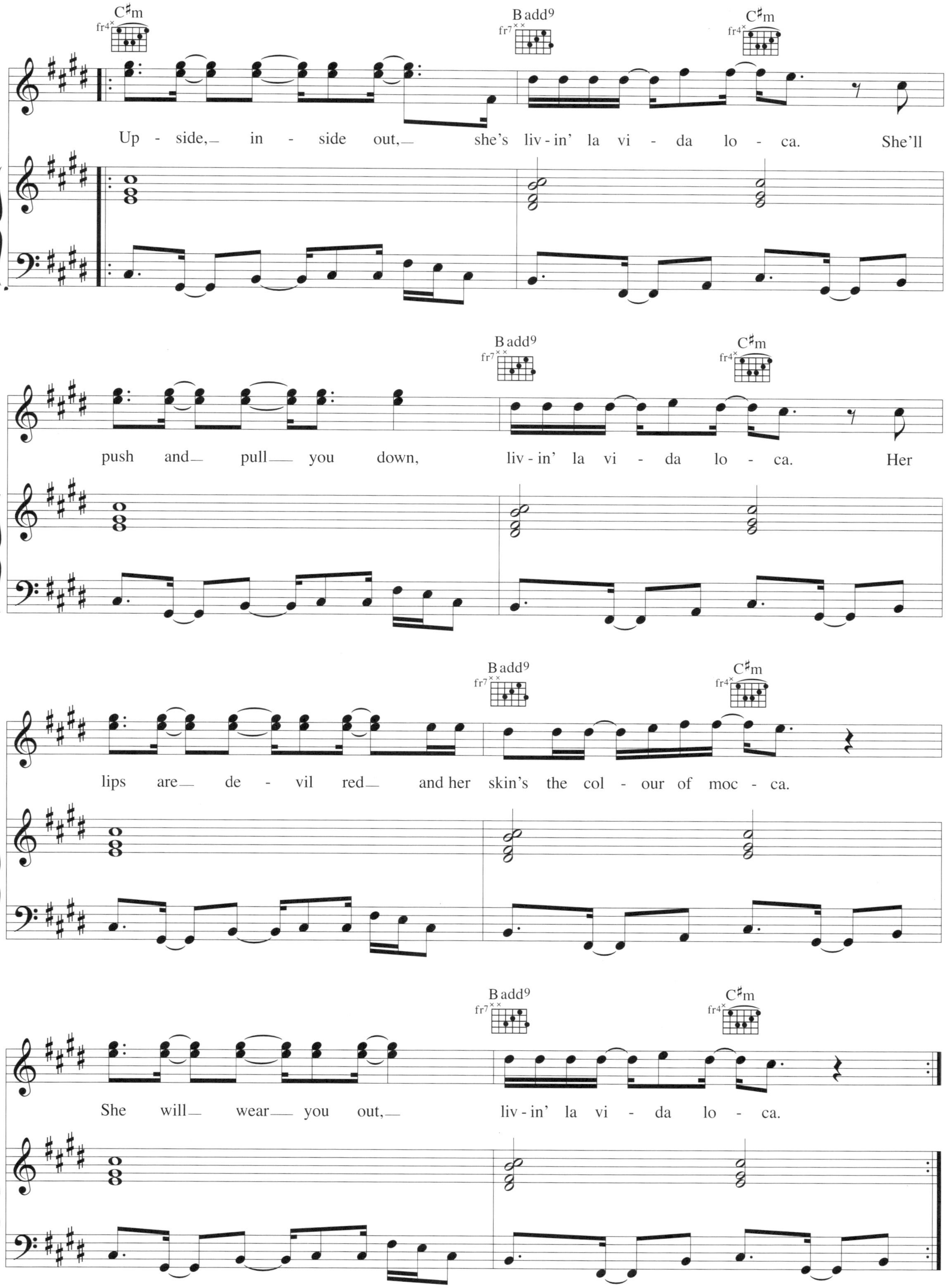
C♯m
Badd9
C♯m
Up - side, in - side out, she's liv - in' la vi - da lo - ca. She'll
Badd9
C♯m
push and pull you down, liv - in' la vi - da lo - ca. Her
Badd9
C♯m
lips are de - vil red and her skin's the col - our of moc - ca.
Badd9
C♯m
She will wear you out, liv - in' la vi - da lo - ca.

Verse 3:
Woke up in New York City
In a funky cheap hotel
She took my heart and she took my money
She must have slipped me a sleepin' pill
She never drinks the water
Makes you order French champagne
And once you've had a taste of her
You'll never be the same
Yeah, she'll make you go insane.

Upside, inside out *etc.*

Lola

Words & Music by Ray Davies

E
walked up to me, and she asked me to dance I
I'm not dumb, but I can't un - der - stand why she
A
D
asked her her name and in a dark brown voice she said
walked like a wo - man and talked like a man oh my
E
A
D
Lo - la El - oh - el - aye Lo - la la la la la
Lo - la la la la la Lo - la la la la la
C
D
E
Lo - la.
Lo - la.,

1.
E
2.
E
Well,
Well we
B7
F♯7
drank cham - pagne and danced all night,
un - der e - lec - tric can - dle light,
she
A
picked me up and sat me on her knee
and said "Dear boy, won't you come home with me?" Well,
E
I'm not the world's most pas - sion - ate guy but when I

A
D
looked in her eyes, well, I al - most fell for my
E
A
D
Lo - la la la la la Lo - la la la la la
C
D
E
Lo - la. Lo - la la la la la
A
D
C
D
Lo la la la la la Lo - la.

E
I
A E B A E B
pushed her a - way, I walked to the door I
A E B E G♯7 4fr C♯m
fell to the floor I got down on my knees then
B B13 E
I looked at her, and she at me. Well, that's the way that I want it to stay, and I

A
D
E
__ al - ways want it to be that way__ for my Lo - la la la__ la la
A
E
Lo - la. Girls will be boys, and boys__ will be girls, it's a
A
D
E
mixed up, mud - dled up, shook up world_ ex - cept for Lo - la la la__ la la
A
B7
Lo - la. Well, I left home just a week be - fore____ and

F♯7
A
I'd ne - ver ev - er kissed a wo - man be - fore, but Lo - la smiled and took me by the hand and
E
said, "Dear boy, I'm gon - na make you a man." Well I'm not the worlds most mas - cu - line man, But I
A
D
E
know what I am, and I'm glad I'm a man and so is Lo - la la la la la
repeat ad lib. to fade
Lo - la la la la la Lo - la.

Lucille

Words & Music by Albert Collins & Richard Penniman

C7
cille, won't you do your sis - ter's
cille, please come back where you be -
cille, ba - by, sat - is - fy my
F7
will? Oh, Lu - cille,
long. Oh, Lu - cille,
heart. Oh, Lu - cille,
C7
won't you do your sis - ter's will?
please come back where you be - long.
ba - by, sat - is - fy my heart.
G7
Well, you ran a - way and left,
I been good to you, ba - by.
I slaved for you, ba - by, and

F7
C7
I love you still.
Please don't leave me a - lone.
gave you such a won - der - ful start.
1,2
3
Lu -
Lu -
I
woke up this morn - ing, Lu - cille was not in sight. I
asked her friends a - bout her, but all their lips were tight. Lu -

F7
cille, please come back where you be -
C7
G7
long. I been good to you, ba - by.
F7
C7
Please don't leave me a - lone.

Louie, Louie

Words & Music by Richard Berry

Medium rock beat

To Coda
Em D A D Em D
oh, ba - by, said we got - ta go.
A
Three
Me
A D Em D A D
fine lit - tle girl is wait - in' for me. Me catch a ship a -
nights and days I sailed the sea. Me think of girl oh
see Ja - mai - ca ah moon a - bove. It won't be long me
Em D A D Em D
- cross the sea. Me sailed that ship ah all a - lone. Me
con - stant - ly. Oh, on that ship I dream she there.
see me love. Me take her in my arms a - gain. I

1, 2.
A D Em D
nev - er think how I'll make it home. Uh
smell the rose ah in her hair. Uh
3.
A D Em D
D.S. al Coda
tell her I'll nev - er leave her here. Uh
Coda
A D Em D A D
we got - ta go. I said we got - ta go now.
Em D A D Em D
Spoken: Take this one outta here.
Shouted: Let's go!

Massachusetts

Words & Music by Barry Gibb, Maurice Gibb & Robin Gibb

E♭
6fr
B♭7
E♭
6fr
home.
And the lights all went
A♭
4fr
To Coda
out in Mas - sa - chu - settes.
The day I
1.
E♭
6fr
B♭7
E♭
6fr
Fm
B♭7
left her stand - ing on her own.
2.
E♭
6fr
B♭7
D.%. al Coda
you.

Verse 2:
Tried to hitch a ride to San Francisco
Gotta do the things I wanna do.
And the lights all went out in Massachusettes
They brought me back to see my way with you

Verse 3:
Talk about the life in Massachusettes
Speak about the people I have seen
And the lights all went out in Massachusettes
And Massachusettes is the one place I have seen.

Mighty Quinn

Words & Music by Bob Dylan

E/G♯ B/F♯ B B7 E B B7 E
Might - y Quinn.
B B7 E B B7 E
1. Ev - 'ry - bo - dy's build - ing ships and boats.
(2.) like to go just like the rest, I like my su - gar sweet, but
3. Let me do what I wan - na do, I can't de - cide 'em all. Just
B B7 E B B7 E
Some are build - ing mo - nu - ments, oth - ers are jot - ting down notes.
jump - ing queues and mak - ing haste just ain't my cup of meat.
tell me where to put 'em and I'll tell you who to call.

B B7 E B B7 E
Ev-'ry-bo-dy's in des-pair, ev-'ry girl and boy. But when
Ev-'ry-one's be-neath the trees, feed-ing pig-eons on a limb. But when
No-bo-dy can get no sleep, there's some-one on ev-'ry one's toes. But when
To Coda
B F♯/A♯ E/G♯ B/F♯
Quinn the Es-ki-mo gets here, ev-'ry-bo-dy's gon-na jump for joy.
Quinn the Es-ki-mo gets here, all the pig-eons gon-na run to him.
Quinn the Es-ki-mo gets here, ev-'ry-bo-dy's gon-na wan-na dose.
B F♯ B F♯/A♯
Come on with-out, come on with-in, you'll not see no-thing like the

1.
E/G♯ B/F♯ B B7 E B B7 E
Might - y Quinn.
2. I
2.
B F♯ B F♯/A♯
Come on with-out, come on with-in, you'll not see no - thing like the
E/G♯ B/F♯
D.S. al Coda
Coda
B
Might - y Quinn.
Come on with - out,
Repeat to fade
F♯ B F♯/A♯ E/G♯ B/F♯
come on with-in, you'll not see no - thing like the Might - y Quinn.

The Model

Words & Music by Ralf Hutter, Karl Bartos & Emil Schult

Am
Em
Am
She plays hard to get, she smiles from
She's play - ing her game, and you can
I saw her on the cov - er of a
Em
Am
Em
time to time.
hear them say:
ma - ga - zine.
It
Now
Am
Em
Am
Em
To Coda
on - ly takes a ca - me - ra to change her mind.
'She is look - ing good, for beau - ty we will pay.'
she's a big suc - cess I want to meet her a - gain.
C
Bm
G

C
Bm
E
1.
2. She's
2.
Am
Em
Am
Em
Am
Em
Am
1.
Em
2.
Em
C
Bm
G

C
Bm
E
D.S. al Coda
3. She's
Coda
Am
Em
Am
Em
Am
Em
Am
Em
Am
Em
Am
Em
Am
Em
Am

Mrs. Robinson

Words & Music by Paul Simon

do do do do.
E
A
D
A/C♯
De de de de de de de de de de de de de.
Bm
F♯
E7
And here's to you

A
F♯m
A
Mis - sus Ro - bin - son,
Je - sus loves you more
(3º see block lyric)
F♯m
D
Bm7
than you will know,
whoa, whoa, whoa.
E
A
God bless you please,
Mis - sus Ro -
F♯m
A
F♯m
- bin - son,
Hea - ven holds a place for those who pray.

D
Bm7
Hey, hey, hey.
Bm
To Coda
F♯7
Hey hey hey.
F♯7
1. We'd like to know a lit-
(Verses 2 & 3 see block lyric)
-tle bit a-bout you for our files.

B7
We'd like to help you learn to help your-
E
- self. Look a-round you, all
A
D
Bm
you need are sym-pa-the-tic eyes.
F♯
Stroll a-round the grounds un-

Verse 2:
Hide it in a hiding place
Where no one ever goes
Put it in your pantry
With your cup cakes
It's a little secret
Just the Robinsons affair
Most of all you've got to hide it from the kids.

Koo koo kachoo Mrs. Robinson *etc.*

Verse 3:
Sitting on a sofa
On a Sunday afternoon
Going to the candidates debate
Laugh about it
Shout about it when you've got to choose
Every way you look at this you lose.

Where have you gone Joe Di Maggio
A nation turns it's lonely eyes to you
Ooh ooh ooh
What's that you say Mrs. Robinson
Jolting Joe has left and gone away
Hey hey hey
Hey hey hey.

My Sweet Lord

Words & Music by George Harrison

F♯m7
B
E
C♯m
4fr
I real - ly want to see you.
know you.
E
C♯m
4fr
Real - ly want to be with you.
Real - ly want to go with you.
E
Real - ly want to see you Lord, but it takes
Real - ly want to show you Lord, that it wonÕt
Fdim
C♯7
F♯m7
B
so long, my Lord.
take long, my Lord.
My sweet Lord,
My sweet Lord,

F♯m7 B F♯m7 B
mm my Lord,
mm my Lord,
F♯m7 B
mm my Lord. I real-ly want to
my sweet Lord. I real-ly want to
E E7
see you. Real-ly want to see you.
C♯7
Real-ly want to see you, Lord. Real-ly want to

F♯
Gdim
D♯7
6fr
see you, Lord, but it takes so long my Lord,
G♯m7
4fr
C♯
my sweet Lord,
mm my Lord,
my, my my Lord,
D.𝄋. and fade
my sweet Lord,

My Way

Original Words & Music by Claude Francois, Jacques Revaux & Gilles Thibaut
English Words by Paul Anka

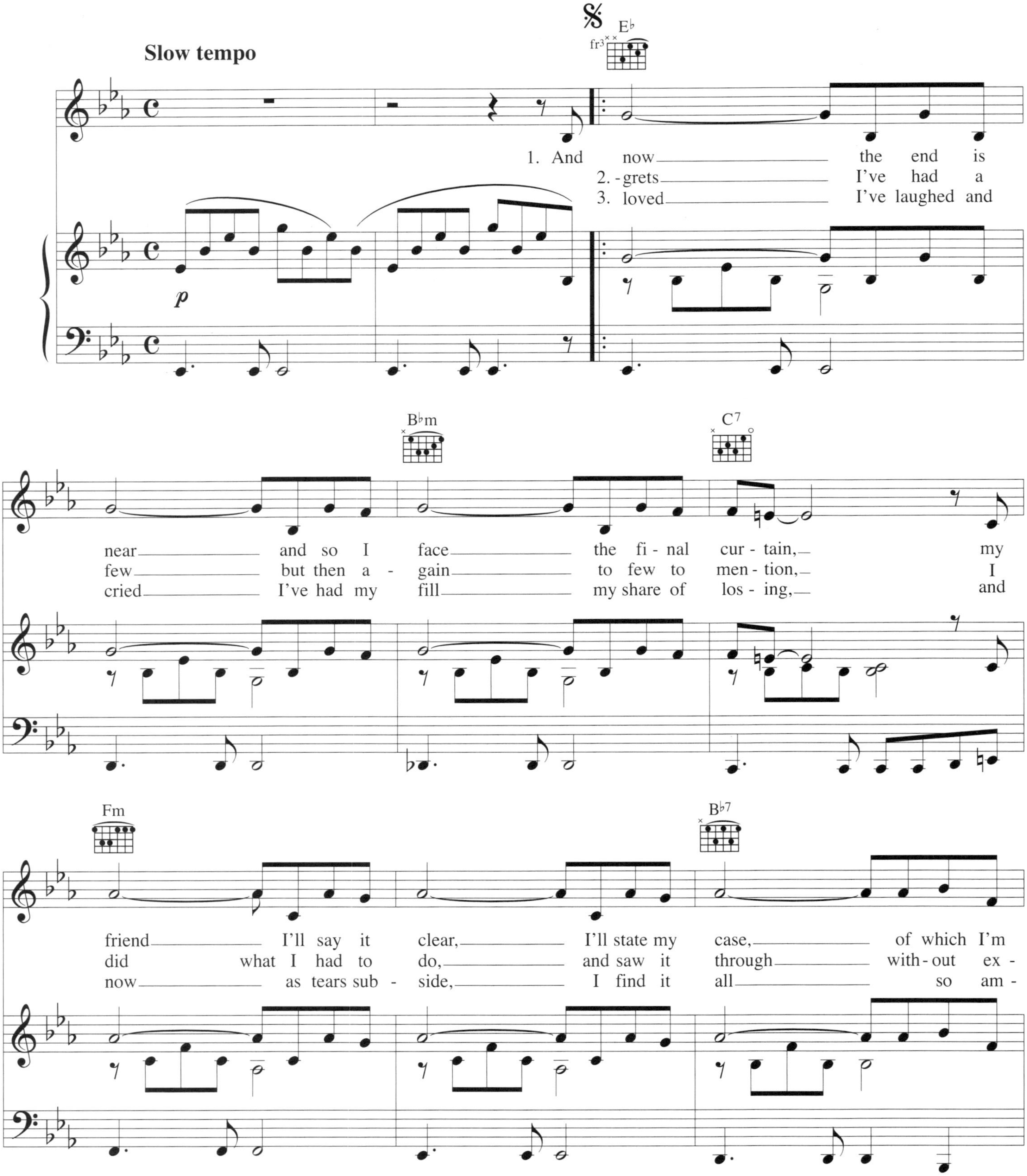

E♭
E♭maj7
B♭m7
E♭7(♭9)
cer - tain. I've lived a life that's full, I've tra - velled
- emp - tion. I planned each char - tered course, each care - ful
- us - ing. To think I did all that and may I
A♭
E♭
each and ev - 'ry high - way, and more, much more than
step a - long the by - way, and more, much more than
say, not in a shy way, oh no, oh no not
Fm7
Fm7
1.
E♭
this, I did it my way. Re -
this, I did it my
me, I did it my
2, 𝄋.
E♭
Gm
E♭
E♭maj7
B♭m7
E♭7(♭9)
way. Yes there were times I'm sure you knew when I bit
way. For what is a man what has he got, if not him -
f

A♭ A♭maj7 A♭ E♭ Fm7
fr4 fr4 fr3
off more than I could chew. But through it all when there was
self then he has not to say the things he'd tru - ly
B♭7 Gm Cm
fr3 fr3
doubt I ate it up and spit it out. I faced it
feel and not the words of one who kneels. The re - cord
Fm B♭7 Fm7 E♭
To Coda
D.%. al Coda
fr3
all and I stood tall and did it my way. I've
shows I took the
p
Coda
B♭7 Fm7 E♭
fr3
blows and did it my way.
rit.
ff

Nights In White Satin

Words & Music by Justin Hayward

C
G
F
Em
Just what the truth is I can't say an - y - more, 'cause I
Just what you want to be, you'll be in the end, and I
A
C
love you, Yes, I love you, Oh, how I
love you, Yes, I love you, Oh, how I
f
cresc.
Em
1.
D
love you.
love you.
ff
2, 3.
D
To Coda
Em
D
How I love you.
mp

C
B
Em
D
mf
C
B
Em
C
Em
C
Am
B
Am
B
Em
D
C
cresc.
Em
D
Em
D
D.%. al Coda
Coda
Em
f
mf

Never Ever

Words & Music by Shaznay Lewis, Esmail Jazayeri & Sean Mather

D♭7
G♭
D♭
or even on the phone, you can write it in a letter, either way I have to know. Did I never treat you right
A♭
G♭
D♭/F
E♭m7
D♭
did I always start the fight? Either way I'm going out of my mind, all the answers to my questions I have to find.
D♭
D♭7
G♭
1. My head's spin - ning, boy I'm in a daze, I feel i - so - lat - ed,
(Verse 2 see block lyric)
D♭
D♭7
don't want to com - mun - i - cate. I'll take a show - er, I will scour, I will run

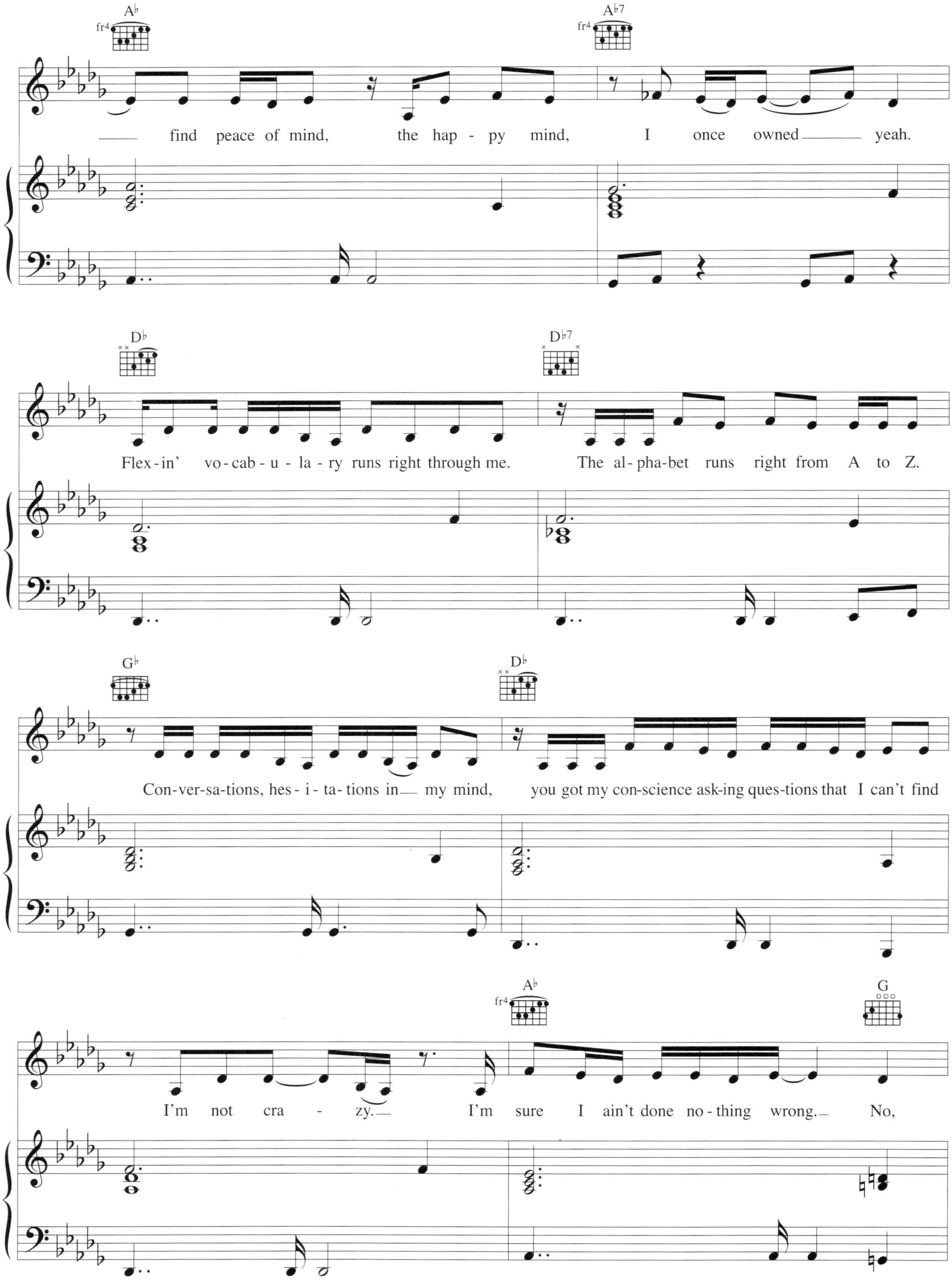
A♭
fr4
A♭7
fr4
find peace of mind, the hap - py mind, I once owned yeah.
D♭
D♭7
Flex-in' vo-cab-u-la-ry runs right through me. The al-pha-bet runs right from A to Z.
G♭
D♭
Con-ver-sa-tions, hes - i - ta-tions in my mind, you got my con-science ask-ing ques-tions that I can't find
A♭
fr4
G
I'm not cra - zy. I'm sure I ain't done no-thing wrong. No,

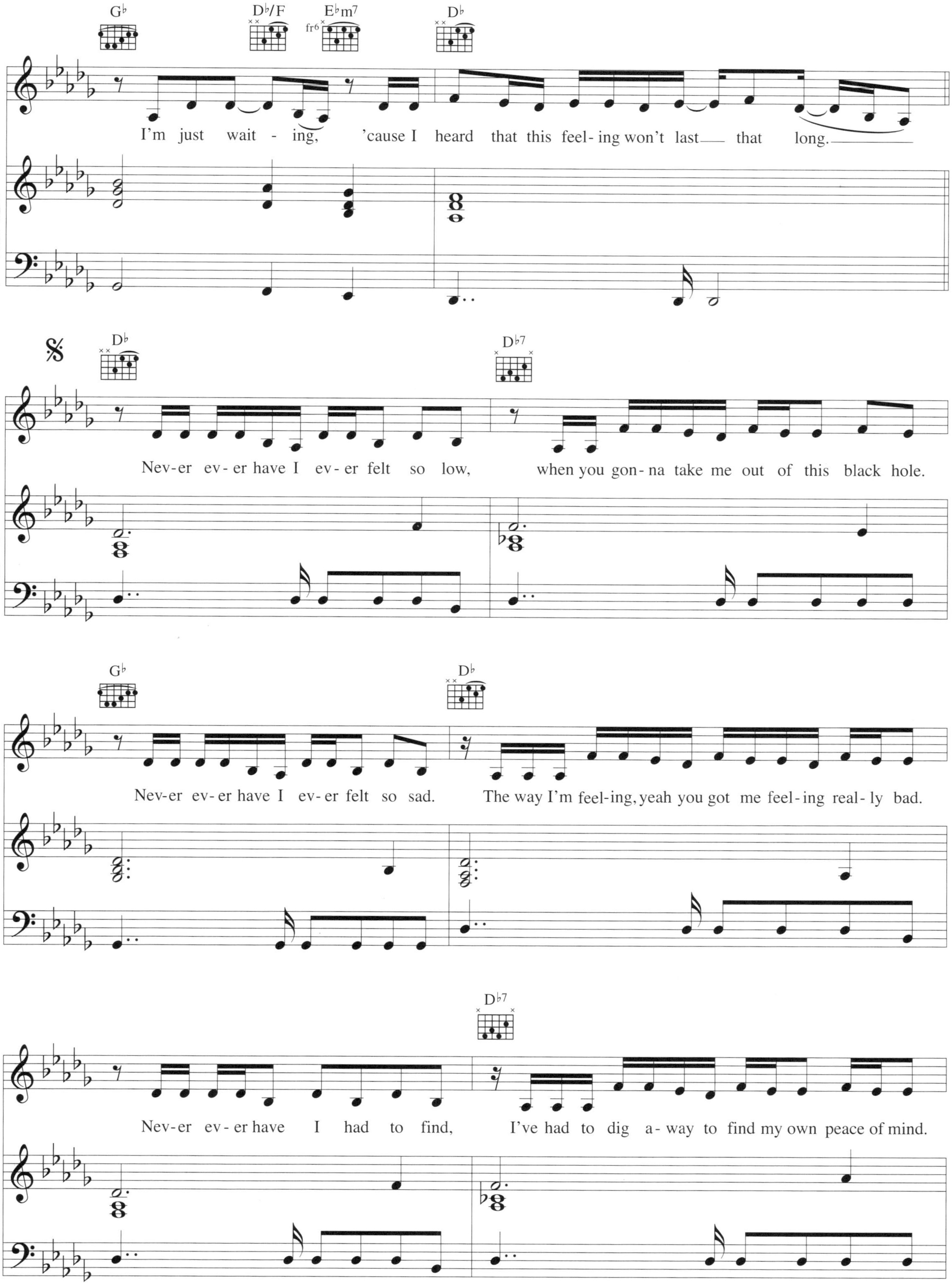

G♭
D♭/F
E♭m7
fr6
D♭
I'm just wait - ing, 'cause I heard that this feel- ing won't last that long.
𝄋
D♭
D♭7
Nev-er ev- er have I ev- er felt so low, when you gon- na take me out of this black hole.
G♭
D♭
Nev-er ev- er have I ev- er felt so sad. The way I'm feel-ing, yeah you got me feel- ing real- ly bad.
D♭7
Nev-er ev- er have I had to find, I've had to dig a- way to find my own peace of mind.

A♭
A♭7
I nev - er ev - er had my con - science to fight, the way I'm feel - ing yeah it just don't feel right.
D♭
Nev - er ev - er have I ev - er felt so low, when you gon - na take me out of this black hole.
G♭
D♭
Nev - er ev - er have I ev - er felt so sad, the way I'm feel - ing, yeah you got me feel - ing real - ly bad.
A♭
G
Nev - er ev - er have I had to find, I've had to dig a - way to find my own peace of mind

Verse 2:
I keep searching deep within my soul
For all the answers, don't wanna hurt no more.
I need peace, got to feel at ease, need to be
Free from pain, go insane, my heart aches.

Sometimes vocabulary runs through my head
The alphabet runs right from A to Z
Conversations, hesitations in my mind.
You got my conscience asking questions that I can't find
I'm not crazy
I'm sure I ain't done nothing wrong
Now I'm just waiting
'Cause I heard that this feeling won't last that long.

Oh, Pretty Woman

Words & Music by Roy Orbison & Bill Dees

F♯m
D
like to meet, pret - ty wo - man,
I don't be -
E
To Coda
lieve you, you're not the truth, no one can look as good as you.
E7

Dm
G
C
Pret - ty wo - man stop a while, pret - ty wo - man
Pret - ty wo - man, yeah yeah yeah, pret - ty wo - man
Am
Dm
G
talk a while, pret - ty wo - man give your smile to
look my way, pret - ty wo - man say you'll stay with
C
1.
2.
A
me.
me. 'Cause I
F♯m
Dm
E
need you, I'll treat you right.

A
F♯m
Dm
Come with me ba - by,
be mine to -
E
D.𝄋. al Coda
night.
Pret-ty
⊕ Coda
hey,
O. K.
if that's the way it must be O. K.

I guess I'll go on home it's late, There'll be to -
mor - row night, but wait, what do I see?
Is she
walk - ing back to me.

Verse 2:
Pretty woman, won't you pardon me?
Pretty woman, I couldn't help but see,
Pretty woman,
That you look lovely as can be,
Are you lonely just like me?

Verse 3:
Pretty woman, don't walk on by,
Pretty woman, don't make me cry,
Pretty woman,
Don't walk away, hey.

Purple Rain

Words & Music by Prince

F
E♭ 6fr
E♭sus4 6fr
E♭ 6fr
I nev - er meant 2 cause u a - ny pain.
All I wan - na be is some kind of friend.
B♭
Gm7 3fr
I on - ly want - ed one time 2 see u laugh - ing. I
Ba - by I could nev - er steal u from an - oth - er.
F
B♭
N.C.
on - ly want - ed to see u laugh - ing in the pur - ple rain.
It's such a shame our friend - ship had 2 end.
Pur - ple rain, pur - ple rain.
E♭ 6fr
E♭sus4 6fr
E♭ 6fr
B♭
Pur - ple rain, pur - ple rain.

Gm7add11
F
Pur - ple rain, pur - ple rain.
Fsus4
F
I on - ly want-ed 2 see u bath - ing
I on - ly want-ed 2 see u un - der -
1.
B♭
N.C.
in the pur - ple rain. 2. I nev - er want-ed 2 be your week - end lov-
-neath the pur - ple
2.
B♭
N.C.
B♭
rain. Hon-ey I know, I know, I know times are chang - ing.

Gm
3fr
F
It's time we all reach out 4 some-thing new:
Eb
6fr
Bb
that means u 2.
You say you want a lead-er,
Gm
3fr
F
but u can't seem to make up your mind.
I think u bet-ter close it,
and let me guide u
Bb
N.C.
2 the pur-ple rain.
Pur-ple rain, pur-ple rain.

E♭
6fr
E♭sus4
6fr
E♭
6fr
B♭
Pur - ple rain, pur - ple rain.
Gm7add11
F
Pur - ple rain pur - ple rain.
B♭
N.C.
On - ly wan - na see u, on - ly wan - na see u in the pur - ple rain.
1, 2.
B♭
Gm
3fr
F
E♭
6fr

3.
E♭
6fr
B♭
Gm
3fr
F
E♭
6fr
B♭
Tacet 1: Ooh ooh ooh
Gm
3fr
F
ooh. Ooh ooh ooh ooh. Ooh ooh ooh
1-5.
E♭
6fr
6.
E♭
6fr
B♭
ooh.
ooh.

Rocket Man

Words & Music by Elton John & Bernie Taupin

Gm9
fr3
I miss the earth so much, I
C9sus4
Am7/C
Gm9
fr3
miss my wife.
It's lone - ly out in space.
C9sus4
B♭/D
E♭
fr3
B♭/D
Cm
fr3
Cm/B♭
fr3
On such a time - - - less flight.
3
F/A
F
F11

B♭
E♭
fr3
And I think it's gon-na be a long, long time 'til touch-down brings me round a-gain to find
B♭
E♭
fr3
B♭/D
I'm not the man I think I am at home.
Oh, I'm a
C
B♭/D
E♭
fr3
rock-et man.
Rock-et man, I'm burn-ing out a fuse up here
B♭
E♭
fr3
a - lone.
3

B♭
E♭
fr3
And I think it's gon-na be a long, long time 'til touch-down brings me round a-gain to find
B♭
E♭
fr3
B♭/D
I'm not the man I think I am at home.
Oh, I'm a
C
B♭/D
E♭
fr3
rock-et man.
Rock-et man, I'm burn-ing out a fuse up here
1.
B♭
E♭
fr3
a-lone.
3

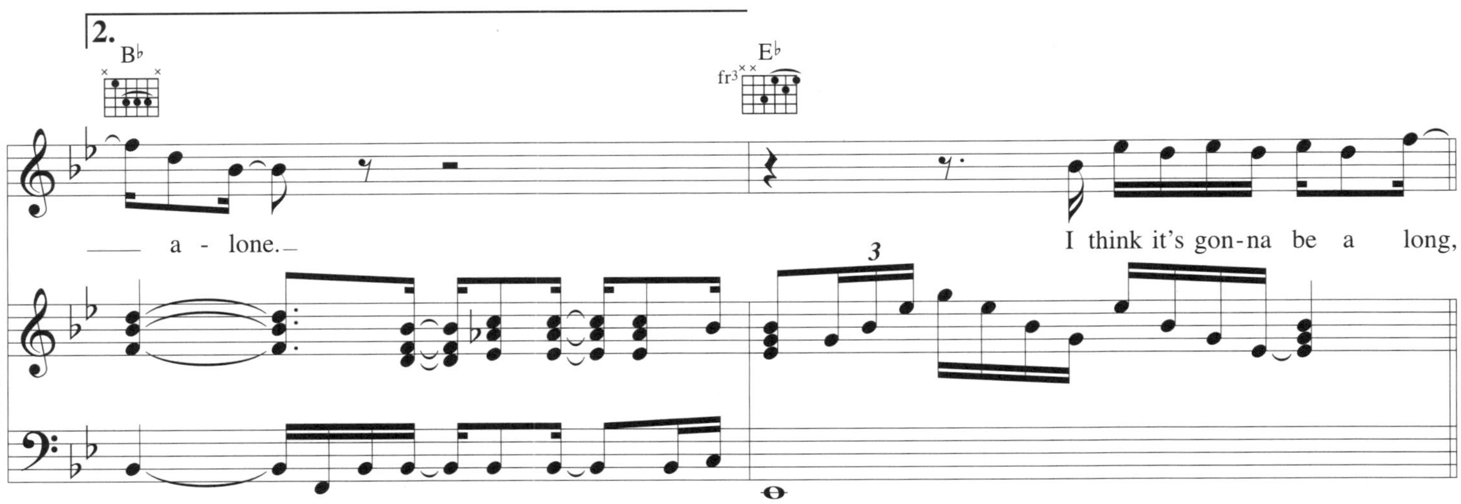

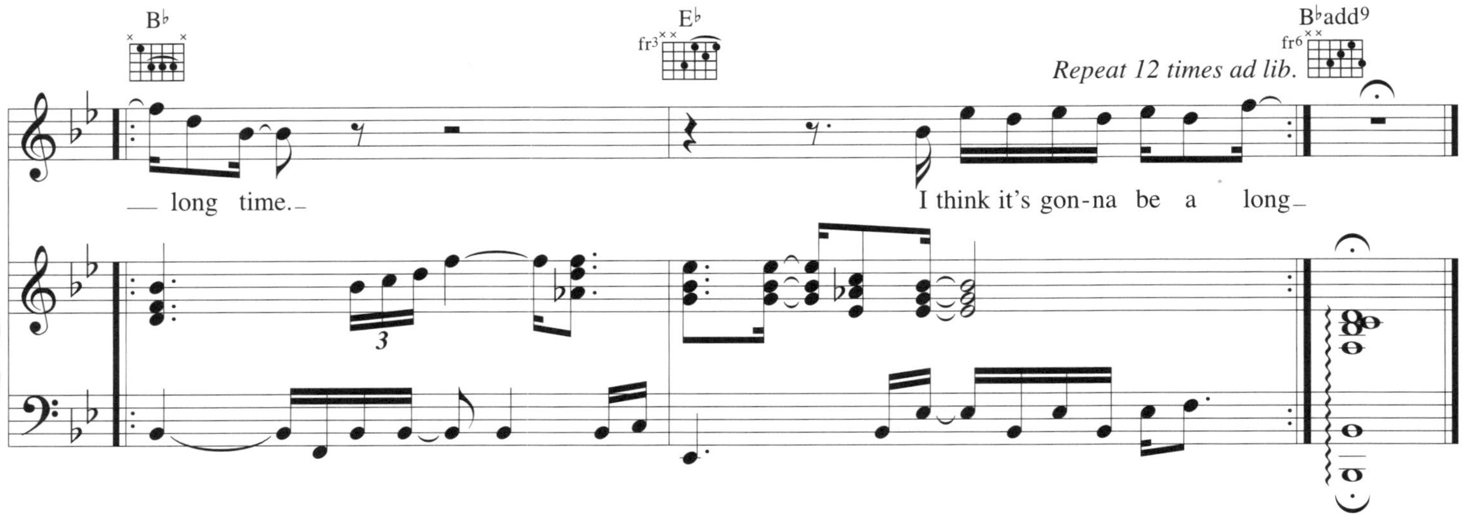

Verse 2:
Mars ain't the kind of place to raise your kids
In fact it's cold as hell
And there's no one there to raise them if you did.
And all this science I don't understand
It's just my job five days a week
A rocket man, oh rocket man.

And I think it's gonna be a long long time *etc.*

Roxanne

Words & Music by Sting

My moves remind me of kung-fu flicks
Thick lips that contradict
rules of the game she plays the politics
red light special, red light kushtie.
Put on your make-up, body all made-up
platinum plate-up, pearl jam put-up
goddam Roxanne, you don't really have to
put on your red dress as if you're feeling kinda rude

she got the hots for the disco jocks
rock the socks at the top of the pops.
Never get through like they call your bluff
twistin' money like... Rox -
E♭maj7
D7 aug
Gm9
fr3
3
- anne, you don't have to put on the red light.
Gm6
E♭maj7
D7 aug
3
Those days are ov - er. You don't have to

Gm9
Gm6
E♭maj7
sell your bo - dy to the night. Rox - anne,
D7 aug
Gm9
Gm6
you don't have to wear that dress to - night,
E♭maj7
D7 aug
walk the streets for mon - ey, you don't
Gm9
Gm6
care if it's wrong or if it's right. Rox - - -

E♭maj7
D7 aug
Gm9
fr3
- anne you don't have to put on the red light,
Gm6
E♭maj7
D7 aug
Rox - - - anne, you don't have to
Gm9
fr3
Gm6
E♭maj7
put on the red light, put on the red light,
D7 aug
Gm9
fr3
Gm6
put on the red light,

E♭maj7
D7 aug
Gm9
fr3
put on the red light,
put on the red light,
Gm6
1.
E♭maj7
D7 aug
put on the red light.
2.
G9
fr4
put on the red light,
put on the red light,

2. *(Rap)*
You with the hat, dancing for the green paperback
Sitting at the bar drinking up Cognac
She stepped in the room, don't know how to act
Sweet in red, she saved my love to save my life
It was the hat, catch, wanna be her xxx
She wants to party, have a good time
She feels kinda hot, needs filling feeling fine
Diggin' all her life just to get a gold mine
Well makin' the streets she's the pippa's paradise
Through the xxx gettin' stoned with the ice
She said I head up the crew, I'm your number one fan
Love the refugees down from the islands
Droppin' the business with her pretty pretty friends
Sippin' colada every day is a weekend.
Heard your name was Pras out of Brooklyn
Inflict a million plays with your total sound scan.

(Sung)
I loved you since I knew you
I wouldn't talk down to you,
I have to tell you just how I feel
I won't share you with another boy.
I know my mind is made up
So put away your make-up
Told you once, I won't tell you again
It's a crime the way…

Roxanne… *etc. as 1º*

Somethin' Stupid

Words & Music by C. Carson Parks

Am7 D7 Am7 D7 Am7 D7
eve - ning with me.__ And if we go some place to dance,_ I
Am7 D7 G G6 Gmaj7 G6
know that there's a chance you won't be leav - ing with me.__ Then
G7 Dm7 G7 C C6
af - ter - wards we drop in - to a qui - et lit - tle place and have a drink or two._
E♭ 6fr Am7 D7 Am7 D7
And then I go and spoil it all_ by say - ing some - thing stu - pid like I

To Coda
Gsus4/2 G G6 Gmaj7 G6 G7 Dm7
love you. I can see it in your eyes you still de-
G7 Cmaj7 C6
-spise the same old lines you heard the night be - fore.
Cmaj9 C6 A7 Em7
And though it's just a line to you, for
D.S. al Coda
A7 D7 Daug
me it's true and nev - er seemed so right be - fore.
2. I

Coda
Gmaj7 G6 G G6 Gmaj7 G6 Am7 D7
Am7 D7 Am7 D7 Am7 D7
G6 G7 Dm7
The time is right, your per - fume fills my
G7 C C6 E♭ 6fr
head, the skies get red and oh, the night's so blue._ And

Verse 2:
I practise every day to find
Some clever lines to say
To make the meaning come true
But then I think I'll wait until
The evening gets late
And I'm alone with you
The time is right
Your perfume fills my head
The stars get red
And oh, the night's so blue
And then I go and spoil it all
By saying something stupid
Like I love you.

Something In The Air

Words & Music by John 'Speedy' Keen

B7sus4
E
E/D
E/C♯
E/B
re - vo - lu - tion's here and you know it's right.
E
E/D
E/C♯
E/B
B7sus4
And you know that it's right. We have got to
get it to - geth - er, we have got to get it to - geth - er
E
E/D
E/C♯
E/B
E
E/D
E/C♯
E/B
now.

F♯
C♯7sus4/F♯
F♯
C♯7sus4
fr4
F♯
C♯7sus4
fr4
Block off the streets and hous - es be-cause there's some-thing in the air.
F♯
We got to get to-geth - er soon-er or lat - er be-cause the
C♯7sus4
fr4
F♯
F♯/E
F♯/D♯
F♯/C♯
re - vo - lu - tion's here and you know it's right.

F♯ F♯/E F♯/D♯ F♯/C♯ C♯7sus4
And you know that it's right. We have got to get it to-geth - er,
C♯m/F♯ D♯m/F♯ C♯m/F♯ D♯m/F♯
we have got to get it to-geth - er now.
C♯m/F♯ D♯m/F♯ C♯m/F♯ D♯m/F♯ E7 E aug E7 E aug E7 E aug E7 E aug
F7 F13 F7 F13 F7 F13 F7 F13 G7 G13

C7
F7
B♭7
F7
B♭7
C7
F7
B♭7
F7
B♭7
F6
F9
F6
F9
B♭
F6
F9
F6
F9
C7
G7
C6/9
C
F13
F7
C6/9
C
F13
F7

C9
A♭
G7
A♭
G7
C9
F7
A♭
A♭
E♭7sus4
A♭
E♭7sus4
A♭
Hand out the arms and am - mo we're gon - na
E♭7sus4
A♭
blast our way through here, we got to get to-geth - er soon-er or lat -

E♭7sus4
- er because the revo - lu - tion's here and you know it's right.
A♭ A♭/G♭ A♭/F A♭/E♭ A♭ A♭/G♭
And you know that it's
A♭/F A♭/E♭ E♭7sus4
right. We have got to get it to - geth - er,
A♭
we have got to get it to - geth - er now.

Son Of A Preacher Man

Words & Music by John Hurley & Ronnie Wilkins

B
cou- sin Bil - ly would take_ me walk - ing,
through the back yard we'd go walk - ing,
not 2°
then he'd look in - to_ my eyes,_
Lord knows to my_ sur - prise._ The
E
A
E
on - ly one_ who could ev - er reach_ me
was the son of a preach - er man._ The
A
E
on - ly boy_ who could ev - er teach_ me
was the son of a preach - er man, yes he

B
A
was he was,
mm, yes he was.
1.
E
2.
D
How well I re - mem - ber
A
the look that was in his eyes,
steal-ing kiss-es from me on the sly,

B
B♭
B
tak-ing time to make_time,
tell-ing me that he's all_ mine,
E7
learn-ing from each oth-er's know-ing,
look-ing to see_how much_we've known_and the
A
D
A
on - ly one_ who could ev - er reach_ me
was the son of a preach-er man. The
A
D
A
on - ly boy_ who could ev - er teach_ me
was the son of a preach-er man, yes he

Verse 2:
Being good isn't always easy
No matter how hard I try.
When he started sweet talking to me,
He'd come and tell me everything is all right,
He'd kiss and tell me everything is all right,
Can't get away again tonight.

Space Oddity

Words & Music by David Bowie

Am
Am/G
D/F♯
take your pro - tein pills and put your hel - met on.
C
Em
Ground Con - trol to Ma - jor Tom,
Ten Nine Eight Seven
C
Em
Am
Am/G
com - menc - ing count - down, en - gines on, check ig - ni - tion and may
Six Five Four Three Two One
D
God's love be with you.
lift-off.
Ped.

C
E7
This is Ground Con - trol to Ma - jor Tom, you've real - ly made the grade
F
Fm
C
and the pa - pers want to know whose shirts you wear.
F
Fm
C
Now it's time to leave the cap - sule if you dare.
F
C
This is Ma - jor Tom to Ground Con - trol,

E7
F
I'm step-ping through the door, and I'm
Fm
C
F
float-ing in a most pe-cu-li-ar way, and the stars
Fm
C
F
look ve-ry dif-fer-ent to-day. For
Fmaj7
Em7
here am I sit-ting in a tin can,
(𝄋) (float-ing round my)

Fmaj7
Em7
far a - bove the world.
(the moon.)
B♭maj9
Am9
fr5
Gadd9
fr3
F
Pla - net Earth is blue and there's no - thing I can do.
C
F
G
A
C
F
G
A
Fmaj7
Em7
A

C/E
F♯7
To Coda
E
C
E7
Though I'm past one hun - dred thou - sand miles I'm feel - ing ve - ry still,
F
Fm
C
and I think my space - ship knows which way to go.
F
Fm
C
Tell my wife I love her ve - ry much, she knows.

F
G
E7(♭9)
Ground Con - trol to Ma - jor Tom, your
Am
Am/G
D7/F♯
cir - cuits dead, there's some - thing wrong, can you hear me Ma - jor Tom, can you
C
G
D.S. al Coda
hear me Ma - jor Tom, can you hear me Ma - jor Tom? Can you
Coda
E
Repeat ad lib. to fade

Suspicious Minds

Words & Music by Francis Zambon

G C/G G C/G G C/G
Why can't you see
C F/C C F/C D G/D
To Coda
what you're do - ing to me,
when you don't be - lieve
C F/C D C G/B D
a word I say?
C G Bm
We can't go on to - geth - er with sus - pi - cious minds.

C D Em Bm7
(Sus - pi - cious minds.) And we can't build our dreams
C D7sus4 D7 D9 B7sus4 B7
1. 2.
4fr
on sus - pi - cious minds. minds.
♪ = 144
Em Bm Bm7 C
Oh, let our love sur - vive, ah, dry the
D Em Bm Bm7
tears from your eyes. Let's don't let a good thing die,

C
D
G
when, ho - ney, you know I'll nev - er lie to you.
Tempo I
C
G
D
D.𝄋. al Coda
Mm. Yeah, yeah.
Coda
D
G/D
C
F/C
G
C/G
when you don't be - lieve a word I say?
G
C/G
G
Oh, don't you know I'm caught in a trap.

Verse 2:
So if an old friend I know, drops by to say hello
Would I still see suspicion in your eyes?
Here we go again, asking where I've been
You can't see the tears are real I'm crying.

We can't go on together, with suspicious minds *etc.*

Verse 3:
We're caught in a trap, I can't walk out
Because I love you too much, baby
Why can't you see what you're doing to me
When you don't believe a word I say?

We can't go on together, with suspicious minds *etc.*

The Tide Is High

Words & Music by John Holt, Howard Barrett & Tyrone Evans

Csus2 F G Csus2
not the things you do that tease and hurt me_ bad, but it's the way you do the things you
(Verse 4 see block lyrics)
F G Csus2 F G
do to me. I'm_ not the kind of girl_ who gives up just_ like
C F G C F G
that,_ oh no_ woh. 3. The tide is_ high but I'm hold - ing on;
C F G C F G
I'm gon - na be your_ num - ber one. The tide is_ high but I'm hold - ing on;

C F G Dm7 G
3fr 3fr 5fr 3fr
I'm gon-na be your num - ber one. Num - ber one.
My num - ber one.
Dm7 G G A
5fr 3fr 3fr
1. 2.
Num - ber one. (Whisper) Number one. one.
D G A
3fr
5. Ev - 'ry time that I get the feel - ing, you give me some - thing to be - lieve in.
D G A
3fr
Ev - 'ry time that I got you near me, I know the way that I want it to be.

D
G
3fr
A
But you know I'm gon - na take my chance now, I'm gon - na make it hap - pen some - how.
D
G
3fr
A
And you know I can take the pres - sure; a mo - ment's pain for a life - time's plea - sure.
N.C.
3
3
Ev - 'ry girl wants you to be her man,
Dsus2
3
but I'll wait right here till it's my turn. I'm not the kind of girl

Verse 4:
Every girl wants you to be her man
But I'll wait right here till it's my turn
I'm not the kind of girl who gives up just like that
Oh no.

Tainted Love

Words & Music by Ed Cobb

With a moving beat

G♯m G♯m/B E C♯m G♯m G♯m/B E C♯m
go no - where, and I've lost my light for I toss
G♯m G♯m/B G♯m
and turn, I can't sleep at night. Once I ran to you, (I
G♯m/B E
ran) now I'll run from you. This taint - ed love you've giv - en, I
C♯m
give you all a boy could give you, Take my tears and that's not liv - in'! Oh,

To Coda
G♯m G♯m/B E C♯m G♯m G♯m/B E C♯m
taint - ed love, taint - ed love.
G♯m G♯m/B E C♯m G♯m G♯m/B E C♯m
Now I know I've got to run a - way, I've got to
G♯m G♯m/B E C♯m G♯m G♯m/B
get a - way. You don't real - ly want an - y - more from me. To make
G♯m G♯m/B E C♯m G♯m G♯m/B E C♯m
things right, you need some - one to hold you tight. And you think
4fr

G♯m G♯m/B E C♯m G♯m G♯m/B
D.S. al Coda
love is to pray, but I m sor - ry, I don t pray that way.
Coda
E C♯m G♯m G♯m/B E C♯m G♯m G♯m/B
Don t touch me, please, I can - not stand the way you
f
E C♯m G♯m G♯m/B E C♯m
tease. I love you tho you hurt me so, now I m
Repeat and fade
G♯m G♯m/B G♯m G♯m/B E C♯m
gon - na pack my things and go. Taint - ed love.
Oh,

Walk On By

Words by Hal David
Music by Burt Bacharach

Am7
Dm7
Am
Make be - lieve that you don't see the tear, just let me breathe in
B♭
Cadd9
F
pri - vate, 'cos each time I see you I break down and cry,
B♭
F
B♭
you walk on by, you walk on by;
F
B♭
F
you walk on by - - - - - ye - ye -
3

F
Am7
D
3
ye.
I just can't get ov - er los - ing you, and so if I seem
Am
D
Am
Gm7
fr3
bro - ken in two,
walk on by,
Am
Gm7
fr3
Am7
walk on by.
Fool - ish pride, that's
Dm7
Am
B♭
all that I have left, so let me hide the tears and the sad - ness you

Cadd9
F
gave me when you said good - bye - - - eye - - eye -
B♭
F
B♭
eye, so walk on by.
So walk on by,
F
B♭
F
you walk on by.
B♭
Am7
Bm
So walk on by,

Am Bm Am Bm Am Bm
Am Gm7 Am
walk on by, walk on by.
Gm Am7 Dm7
Fool - ish pride, that's all that I have left, so
Am B♭ Cadd9
let me hide the tears and the sad - ness you gave me when you said good -

F
B♭
bye - - eye eye - eye, so walk on by,
F
B♭
F
so walk on by.
B♭
F
Now you real - ly got - ta go, so walk on by.
2º fade
B♭
F
B♭
Take your leave, you'll ne - ver see those tears that cry.

With A Little Help From My Friends

Words & Music by John Lennon & Paul McCartney

A C♯m/G♯ Bm/F♯ Bm E7 A
4fr
What would you do if I sang out of tune?
Would you stand up and walk out on me?
A C♯m/G♯ Bm/F♯ Bm
4fr
3
Lend me your ears and I'll sing you a song.
E7 A
I will try not to sing out of key, yeah, oh ba - by.
G D/F♯ A G D/F♯ A
(By with a lit - tle help from my friends.)
(Ad lib. response)
(High with a lit - tle help from my friends.)
(Ad lib. response)

G D/F# A G D/F# A
(Try with a lit-tle help from my friends.)
(Ad lib. response)
(Ooh, ooh, ooh.)
A C#m/G# Bm/F# Bm E7 A
4fr
What do I do when my love is a-way? (Does it wor-ry you to be a-lone?) No, no.
A C#m/G# Bm/F# Bm E7 A
4fr
How do I feel at the end of the day? Are you sad 'cause you're on your own?)
(Ad lib. response)
G D/F# A G D/F# A
(By with a lit-tle help from my friends.)
(High with a lit-tle help from my friends.)

G D/F♯ A G D/F♯ A
(Try with a lit - tle help from my friends.) (Ooh, ooh, ooh.)
N.C. F♯m
(Do you need a - ny - bo - dy?)
A N.C. F♯m
I need some - one to love.
(Could it be a - ny - bo - dy?) All I need is
(2° ad lib.)
E
some - one; not just where I'm go - ing,

N.C.
some - bo - dy knows what I'm show - ing. Ba - by.
G D/F♯ A G D/F♯ A
(By with a lit - tle help from my friends.) (High with a lit - tle help from my friends.)
G D/F♯ A To Coda G D/F♯ A
(Try with a lit - tle help from my friends.) (Ooh, ooh, ooh.)
A C♯m/G♯ Bm/F♯ Bm E7 A
4fr
(Would you be - lieve in a love at first sight?) I'm cer - tain it hap - pens all the time, yeah.

A C#m/G# Bm/F# Bm E7 A
D.S. al Coda
(What do you see when you turn out the light?) I can't tell you, but it sure feels like my life.
Coda G/A D/F# A G/A D/F# A
(By with a lit-tle help from my friends.) (High with a lit-tle help from my friends.)
G/A D/A A
(Try with a lit - tle help from my friends.)
G/A D/A A G/A D/A A
Repeat to fade
(Ooh, ooh, ooh.)

Yellow

Words & Music by Guy Berryman, Jon Buckland, Will Champion & Chris Martin

Guitar Tuned:

① = D♯ ④ = B
② = B ⑤ = A
③ = G ⑥ = E

B
fr7
F♯6
fr2
1. Look at the stars, look how they shine for you,
Emaj7
and ev-'ry-thing you do.
Yeah, they were all yel-low.
B
fr7
F♯6
fr2
I came a-long, I wrote a song for you,
(Verse 2 see block lyric)
Emaj7
and all the things you do.

B
Badd11
And it was called yel-low.
So then I took my
F♯6
Emaj7
turn,
oh, what a thing to've done.
B
Badd11
B
And it was all yel-low.
Emaj7
G♯m6
F♯6
Emaj7
Your skin, oh yeah, your skin and bones turn in -

G♯m6
F♯6
Emaj7
- to some-thing beau - ti - ful.
And you know,
G♯m
F♯6
Emaj7
E add9
you know I love you so.
You know I love you so.
B
B add11
F♯6
Emaj7

1.
2.
B
Badd11
Badd11
It's
B
Badd11
F♯6
true,
look how they shine for
you.
Emaj7
Look how they shine for
you.
Look how they shine for.
B
Badd11
F♯6
Look how they shine for
you,

Verse 2:
I swam across, I jumped across for you
Oh, what a thing to do
Cos you were all yellow
I drew a line, I drew a line for you
Oh, what a thing to do
And it was all yellow.

Your skin, oh yeah, your skin and bones
Turn into something beautiful
And you know, for you I'd bleed myself dry
For you I'd bleed myself dry.

The Whole Of The Moon

Words & Music by Mike Scott

C
G/C
fr3
C
I pic - tured a rain - bow,
you
G/C
fr3
F
Em7/F
held it in your hands.
I had flash - es,
3
F
Em7/F
C
but you saw the plan.
I wand - ered out in the
(2° see block lyric)
G/C
fr3
C
G/C
fr3
world for years,
while you just stayed in your

F
Em7/F
F
room. I saw the crescent,
Em7/F
C
G/C
fr3
you saw the whole of the moon. The whole of the
F
Em7/F
To Coda
C
moon. Ooh, you were there in the turnstiles, with the
G/C
fr3
C
G/C
fr3
wind at your heels. You stretched for the stars and you know how it feels to reach

F
Em7/F
F
too high, too far, too soon.
Em7
C
G/C
fr3
You saw the whole of the moon. I was ground - ed
C
G/C
fr3
F
while you filled the skies. I was dumb - found-
Em7/F
F
Em7/F
- ed by truth, you cut through lies.

C
G/C
fr3
I saw the rain - dir - ty val - ley,
(moon) 2° Instrumental
C
G/C
fr3
Fmaj7
3
you saw Bri - ga - doon.
I saw the cres - cent,
Em7/F
Fmaj7
1.
Em7/F
you saw the whole of the
2.
Em7/F
C
G/B
I spoke a - bout the wings,

Am7
G
F
you just flew.
I won - dered,
I guessed and I
tried.
C/E
Dm7
Em7
You just knew
I
C
G/C
C
sighed,
but
G/C
F
Em7/F
you swooned.
I saw the cres-cent,

F
Em7/F
C
you saw the whole of the moon.
G/C
fr3
F
Em7/F
D.%. al Coda
The whole of the moon.
With a
Coda
C
G/C
fr3
u-ni-corns and can-non balls, pa-la-ces and piers.
C
G/C
fr3
Trum-pets, towers and te-ne-ments, wide o-ceans full of tears.

F
Em7/F
F
Flags, rags, fer-ry boats, sci-mi-tars and scarves. Ev-'ry pre-cious dream and vi-sion
Em7/F
C
G/C
fr3
un-der-neath the stars. Yes, you climbed on the lad-der with the wind in your sails. You
C
G/C
fr3
F
came like a com-et, blaz-ing your trail. Too high,
Em7/F
F
Em7/F
too far, too soon. You saw the whole of the

2°:
With a torch in your pocket
And the wind at your heels
You climbed on the ladder
And you know how it feels to get too high
Too far
Too soon
You saw the whole of the moon
The whole of the moon.

11/03 (49478)